Goldwin Smith

False Hopes

Or Fallacies Socialistic and Semi-Socialistic, Briefly Answered

Goldwin Smith

False Hopes
Or Fallacies Socialistic and Semi-Socialistic, Briefly Answered

ISBN/EAN: 9783337085261

Printed in Europe, USA, Canada, Australia, Japan

Cover: Foto ©Suzi / pixelio.de

More available books at **www.hansebooks.com**

FALSE HOPES:

OR

' FALLACIES, SOCIALISTIC AND SEMI-SOCIALISTIC,

BRIEFLY ANSWERED.

An Address.

BY

GOLDWIN SMITH, D. C. L.

NEW YORK:

JOHN W. LOVELL COMPANY,

TORONTO: WILLING & WILLIAMSON.

1883.

FALSE HOPES:

OR, FALLACIES, SOCIALISTIC AND SEMI-SOCIALISTIC, BRIEFLY EXAMINED.

THE belief that the lot of man can be equalized by economical change, and the desire to make the attempt, are at present strong: they are giving birth to a multitude of projects, and in Europe are threatening society with convulsions. Eagerness to grasp a full share of the good things of this world has been intensified by the departure, or decline, of the religious faith which held out to the unfortunate in this life the hope of indemnity in another. " If to-morrow we die, and death is the end, to-day let us eat and drink; and if we have not the wherewithal, let us see if we cannot take from those who have." So multitudes are saying in their hearts, and philosophy has not yet furnished a clear reply. Popular education has gone far enough to make the masses think—not far enough to make them think deeply; they read what falls in with their aspirations, and their minds run in the groove thus formed; flattering theories make the rapidly, and, like religious doctrines, are imbibed without examination by credulous and uncritical minds. The numbers of Communists, or Socialists, in any country, is as yet small, compared with that of the population at large; yet the doctrines spread, chiefly among the artisan class, which is active-minded, is gathered in commercial centres, lives on wages about the rate of which there are frequent disputes, is filled with the thirst of pleasure by ever-present temptations, and stirred to envy by the perpetual sight of wealth. Envy is a potent factor in the movement, and is being constantly inflamed by the ostentation of the vulgar rich, who thus deserve, fully as much as the revolutionary artisans, the name of a dangerous class. This is the main source of that' extreme sort of Communism which may be called Satanism, as it seeks, not to reconstruct, but to destroy and to destroy not only existing institutions, but established morality—social, domestic, and personal—putting evil in place of good. Satanism manifests itself in different countries under various forms and names—such as Nihilism, Intransigentism, Petrolean Communism, the Dynamite wing of Fenianism ; Nihilism being defined with more startling sharpness than the

* One of the French Communists, it seems, rejoices in the name Lucifer Satan Vercingetorix.

rest, though the destructive spirit of all is the same. Social innovation is everywhere more or less allied with, and impelled by, the political and religious revolution which fills the civilized world; while the revolution in science has helped to excite the spirit of change in every sphere, little as Utopianism is akin to science.

No man, with a brain and a heart, can fail to be penetrated with a sense of the unequal distribution of wealth, or to be willing to try any experiment which may hold out a reasonable hope of putting an end to poverty. By the success of such an experiment, the happiness of the rich—of such, at least, of them as are good men—would be increased far more than their riches would be diminished. But only the Nihilists would desire blindly to plunge society into chaos. It is plainly beyond our power to alter the fundamental conditions of our being. There are inequalities greater even than those of wealth, which are fixed not by human lawgivers but by nature such as those of health, strength, and intellectual power; and these, almost inevitably, draw other inequalities with them. The most violent shocks given to the social system— such as the French Revolution—have overturned unjust governments and laws, though at the immediate cost of much confusion, impoverishment, and suffering; but they have failed materially to diminish the inequalities of wealth, as the French Communists themselves, by their passionate complaints, declare. Injustice is human, and where inequality is the fiat, not of man, but of a power above man, it is idle, for any practical purpose, to assail it as injustice. The difference between a good and a bad workman is, partly at least, the act of nature; and to give the same wages to the good workman and the bad, as Communists propose, might be just from some superhuman point of view: from the only point of view to which humanity can attain, it would be unjust.

The plans of innovation proposed vary much in character and extent. Those which here will be briefly passed in review are Communism, Socialism, Nationalization of Land, Strikes, plans for emancipating Labor from the dominion of Capital, and theories of innovation with regard to Currency and Banks, the most prominent of which is Greenbackism, or the belief in paper money. This seems a motley group, but it will be seen on examination, that there runs through the whole the same hope of bettering the condition of the masses without increase of industry, or of the substantial elements of wealth. Through several there runs a tendency to violence and confiscation. It may be safely said, that all the movements draw their adherents from minds of the same speculative class, and that industrial revolution is not often recruited from the ranks of steady and prosperous industry.

By Communism is here meant the proposal to abrogate altogether the institution of property. The reply is that property is not an institution but a fixed element of human nature. A state of things in which a man would not think that what he had made for himself was his own, is unknown to experience and beyond the range of our conceptions. The author of the saying that property is theft affirmed, by his use of the word theft, the rightful existence of property, and it is highly probable that as a literary man he would have asserted his claim to copyright, which is property in its subtlest form. In early times property in land was not individual but tribal; it is so still in Afghanistan, while in Russia and Hindostan it is vested in the village community which assigns lots to the individual cultivators: still it is property: squat upon the land of an Afghan tribe, or of a village community, Russian or Hindoo, in the name of humanity, and you will be ejected as certainly as if you had squatted on the land of an English Squire. In primitive hunting-grounds and pastures, property was less definite; yet even these would have been defended against a rival tribe. Property in clothes, utensils, arms, must always have been individual. Declare that everything belongs to the community; still government must allot each citizen his rations; as soon as he receives them the rations will be his own, and if another tries to take them he will resist, and by his resistance affirm the principle of individual property.

Religious societies, in the fervor of their youth, have for a short time sought to seal the brotherhood of their members by instituting within their own circle a community of goods. The primitive Christians did this, but they never thought of abolishing property or proclaiming the communistic principle to society at large. Paul, in is Epistles, on the contrary, distinctly ratifies the ordinary principle of industry. " While the land remained," says Peter to Ananias, " did it not remain thine own; and after it was sold was it not in thy power ? " Christian communism, so-called, was in fact merely a benefit fund or club: it was also short-lived ; as was the communism of the Monastic orders, which soon gave way to individual. proprietorship on no ordinary scale in the persons of the abbots.

Associations, called communistic, have been founded in the United States. But these have been nothing more than common homes for a small number of people, living together as one household on a joint-stock fund. Their relations to the community at large have been of the ordinary commercial kind. The Oneida Community owned works carried on by hired labor and dealt with the outside world like any other manufacturer; nor did it make any attempt to propagate communistic opinions. A religious dictatorship seems essential to the unity and peace of these households; but where they have prospered economically, the secret of their success has been the absence of children, which limited their expenses and enabled them to save money. Growing wealthy they have ceased to proselytize, and, if celibacy was kept up, have become tontines. They afford no proof whatever of the practicability of communism as a universal system.

Slavery has its whip; but, saving this, no general incentive to labor other than property has yet been devised. Communists think that they can rely on love of the community, and they point to the case of the soldier who they say does his duty voluntarily from a sense of military honor. It is replied that so far from being voluntary, a soldier's duty is prescribed by a code of exceptional severity, enforced by penalties of the sternest kind.

That the family and all its affections are closely bound up with property is evident ; and the Nihilist is consistent in seeking to destroy property and the family together.

Tracing property to its source, we find it has its origin, as a general rule, not in theft but in labor, either of the hand or of the brain, and in the frugality by which the fruits of labor have been saved. In the case of property which has been inherited, we may have to go back generations in order to reach this fact, but we come to the fact at last. Wherever the labor has been honest, good we may be sure has been done, and the wealth of society at large, as well as that of the worker, has been increased in the process.   Some property has, of course, been acquired by bad means, such as stock-jobbing or gambling; and if we could only distinguish this from the rest, confiscation might be just; for there is nothing sacred in property apart from the mode in which it has been acquired. But discrimination is impossible : all that we can do is to discourage as much as possible bad modes of acquisition.   Hereditary wealth, owned by those who have themselves not worked for it, strikes us as injustice.   But what can be done ?   Bequest is merely a death-bed gift: if we forbid a man to bequeath his wealth, he will give it away in his lifetime, rather than leave it to be confiscated, and a great inducement to saving will be lost.

That wealth is often abused, fearfully abused, is too true : so are strength, intellect, power and opportunities of all kinds.   It is also true that nothing can be more miserable, or abject, than to live in idleness by the sweat of other men's brows. But this is felt, in an increasing degree, by the better natures; private fortunes are held more and more subject to the claims of the community: a spontaneous communism is thus making way, and notably, as every observer will see, in the United States. In the meantime, though the sight of wealth, no doubt, adds a moral sting to poverty, its increase, instead of aggravating, improves the lot even of the poorest. In wealthy communities, the destitute are relieved: in the savage state they die.

By Socialism is meant the theory of those who for free markets, competition, liberty of private contract, and all the present agencies of commerce, propose in various degrees to introduce the regulation and payment of industry by " the State." What is the State? People seem to suppose that there is something outside and above the members of the community which answers to this name, and which has duties and a wisdom of its own. But duties can attach only to persons, wisdom can reside only in brains. The State, when you leave abstractions and come to facts, is nothing but the government, which can have no duties but those which the Constitution assigns it, nor any wisdom but that which is infused into it by the mode of appointment or election. What, then, is the government which Socialism would set up, and to which it would intrust powers infinitely greater than those which any ruler has ever practically wielded, with duties infinitely harder than those which the highest political wisdom has ever dared to undertake? This is the first question which the Socialist has to answer. His school denounces all existing governments, and all those of the past, as incompetent and unjust. What does he propose to institute in their room, and by what process. elective or of any other kind, is the change to be made? Where will he find the human ma-terial out of which he can frame this earthly Providence, infallible and incorruptible, whose award shall be unanimously accepted as superior to all existing guarantees for industrial justice? The chiefs of industry are condemned before-hand as tyrannical capitalists. Will the artisan submit willingly to the autocratic rule of his brother? This question, once more, presents itself on the threshold and demands an answer. To accept an unlimited and most searching despotism without knowing in whose hands it is to be entrusted would evidently be sheer mad-ness. It is idle to form theories, whether economical or social, without considering the actual circumstances under which they are to be applied, and the means and possibilities of carrying them into effect.

Despotic the Socialist's government must be, in order to secure submission to its assignment of industrial parts and to its award of wages, which are not to be measured by the amount or quality of the work, but by some higher law of benevolence, as well as to enable it to compel indolence to work at all. Its power, practically, must be made to extend beyond the sphere of industry to those of social, domestic and individual life. Resistance to its decrees could not be permitted, nor could it be deposed in case of tyranny or abuse. Liberty, in short, would be at an end, and with liberty progress. All Utopias are assumed by their inventors to be the last birth of time.

Assignment of manual labor and payment for its performance by a paternal government are conceivable, though not practically feasible. But how could men be told off for intellectual labor, for scientific research, for invention?

Could the Socialistic ruler pick out a Shakespeare, a Newton, or an Arkwright, set him to his work and pay him while he was about it? Socialism would be barbarism. Of the artisans who applaud these theories all whose trades minister to literature, art, or refinement would be in danger of finding themselves without work.

Socialists often propose to cut up the industrial and commercial world into phalansteries, or sections of some kind, for the purposes of their organization. But industry and commerce are networks covering the whole globe. To what phalanstery would the sailors, the railway men, and the traders between different countries, be assigned?

Take any complex product of human labor, say, a piece of cotton goods worth a cent. Let the Socialist trace out, as far as thought will go, the industries which, in various ways,

and in different parts of the world, have con-
tributed to the production, including the making of machinery, ship-building, and all the
employments and branches of trade ancillary to
these: let him consider how, by the operation
of economic law, under the system of industrial
liberty, the single cent is distributed among all
these industries justly, "even to the estimation
of a hair," and then let him ask himself whether
his government, or his group of governments,
is likely to do better than nature.   If it does, it
will, indeed, be a miracle of political construc-
tion.

The action of government in regard to industry has been of late a good deal enlarged in
the way of Factory Acts, sanitary regulations,
and provisions for the safety of workmen. Pos·
sibly it may be susceptible of still further
enlargement, with benefit to the community.
But at each step you incur, especially under

the elective and party system, new dangers of error, abuse, and corruption. Division of labor, as Adam Smith has shown, marks the progress of civilization; and a centralization, which should reduce all functions to those of a single organ, would be not an advance, but a degradation, in the political as in the animal world. The National workshops at Paris were a complete failure, and even the Government dockyards in England, though rendered necessary by the exigencies of national defence, are conducted less economically than private ship-yards.

A special form of Socialism is Agrarianism, which demands the Nationalization of Land. This has received an impulse from recent legislation for Ireland. Not that the Irish tenant farmer is an agrarian socialist, or a socialist of any kind: what he wants is to oust the landlord, and have the farm to himself; if you demand, as a member of the community, a share of his land, he will give you six feet of it; he exacts a heavy rent for a little croft from the farm laborer in his employment. The sirens of Nationalization have sung to him in vain. Nor did the framers of the Land Act intend to abrogate or assail private property in land: they intended only to adjust by legislation a dispute between two classes of property-holders which threatened the peace of the State. But the natural consequences have been a general disturbance of ideas, and an increase of hope and activity among the apostles of agrarian plunder.

By these theorists it is proposed to confiscate, either openly, or under the thin disguise of a predatory use of the taxing power, every man's freehold, even the farm which the settler has just reclaimed by the sweat of his own brow from the wilderness; and it is emphatically added, with all the exultation of insolent injustice, that no compensation is to be allowed. That the State has, by the most solemn and repeated guarantees, ratified private proprietorship and undertaken to protect it, matters nothing; nor even that it has itself recently sold the land to the proprietor, signed the deed of sale, and received the payment. That such views can be propounded anywhere but in a robber's den or a lunatic asylum, still more, that they can find respectful hearers, is a proof that the economical world is in a state of curious perturbation.

In the first place, how do the Nationalizers mean to carry into effect their schemes of confiscation? They can hardly suppose that large classes will allow themselves to be stripped of all they possess, and turned out with their wives and children to beggary, without striking a blow for their freeholds. There

will at once be civil war, in which it is by
no means certain that the agrarian philosopher
and his disciples would get the better of
the owners and tillers of land. Utopians forget
that they have to deal with the world as it
is.

In the second place, as it is to the government that all land, or the rent of all land, is
to be made over, we must ask the agrarian
socialist, as well as the general socialist, what
form of government he means to give us? The
theorists themselves denounce, as loudly as any
one, the knavery and corruption of the politicians, who would hardly be made pure and
upright simply by putting the management
of fabulous revenues into their hands. Paying
rent for all real estate to the Bosses would certainly be a singular way of regenerating society.
Once more, then, what is the form of government which the Nationalizers have in view?

It would be instructive, if they could furnish us, at the same time, with a sketch of the Land Department of the future, with its staff, the use which it will make of its funds, and the means by which it will be controlled and guarded against corruption.

Why is property in land thus singled out for forfeiture; and why are its holders selected for robbery and denunciation? Because, say the Nationalizers, the land is the gift of God to mankind, and ought not to be appropriated by any individual owner. This would preclude appropriation by a nation, as well as appropriation by a man; but let that pass. In every article which we use, in the paper and type of the very book which advocates confiscation, there are raw materials and natural forces, which are just as much the gift of God as the land. God made the wool of which your coat is woven to grow on the sheep's back, and

endowed steam with the power to work the
engine of the mill.   Land is worth nothing, it
is worth no more than the same extent of sea,
till it is brought under cultivation by labor,
which must be that of particular men.   This,
Canadian Colonization Companies are learning
to their cost.   If the State, in resuming posses-
sion of the land, were compelled, like a landlord in Ireland, to give compensation for im-
provements, it would have to pay the full value
of the land.   The value is the creation of individual labor and capital, in this case, as in the
case of a manufacture.   Circumstances, such
as the growth of neighboring cities, may favor
the landowner.   Circumstances may favor any
owner or producer.   They may also be un-
favorable to any owner or producer, as they
have been of late to the landowners and agri-.
cultural producers in England ; and unless the
State means to protect the holder of property

against misfortune it has surely no right to mulct him for his good luck.

Nor is there anything specially unjust, or, in any way peculiar, about the mode in which the laborer on land is paid by the landowner or capitalist. Every laborer draws his pay from the moment when he begins his work. He draws it in credit, which enables him to get what he wants at the store, if not at once in cash.

All land will, of course, fall under the same rule. The lot on which the mechanic has built his house, will be confiscated as well as the ranch. Not only so, but the produce, being equally with the land the gift of the Creator, will be exempt from the possibility of lawful ownership, and we shall be justified in repudiating our milk bills because cows feed on grass.

Is Poverty the offspring of land-ownership or

the land laws? Any one who is not sailing
on the wings of a theory can answer that
question by looking at the facts before his
eyes. Poverty springs from many sources, personal and general,—from indolence, infirmity,
age, disease, intemperance; from the failure
of harvests and the decline of local trade; from
the growth of population beyond the means of
subsistence. If the influence of the last cause
is denied, let it be shown what impelled the
migrations by which the earth has been peo-
pled. Poverty has existed on a large scale
in great commercial cities, which the land laws
could but little affect, and even in cities like
Venice, which had no land at all. The sup-
posed increase of poverty itself is a fiction;
at least, it is a fallacy. The number of people,
in all civilized countries, living in plenty and
comfort, has multiplied a hundredfold; and
though, with a vast increase in numbers, there is

necessarily a certain increase of misfortune, even the poorest are not so ill off now as they were in the times of primitive barbarism, when famine stalked through the unsettled tribes, though there was no " monopoly " of land.

We cannot all be husbandmen or personally make any use of land. What we want, as a community, is that the soil shall produce as much food as possible, so that we may all live in plenty; and facts, as well as rea-- son, show that a high rate of production can be attained only where tenure is secure. The greater the security of tenure, the more of his labor and capital the husbandman will put into the land, and the larger the harvest will be. The spur which proprietorship lends to industry, is proverbially keen in the case of ownership of land. Originally, all ownership was tribal; and if tribal ownership has, in all civilized countries, given place to private ownership, this is the verdict of experience in favor of the present system. To suppose that a company of land-grabbers aggressed upon the public property, and set up a monopoly in their own favor, is a fancy as baseless as the figments of Rousseau. That we have all a right to live upon the land, is a proposition, in one sense, absurd, unless the cities are to be abandoned, and we are to revert to the normal state; in another sense, true, though subject to the necessary limit of population. But 'what the Nationalizers practically propose is, that a good many of us, instead of living, shall, by reduced production, be deprived of bread and die. The first consequence of their universal confiscation will be a universal disturbance of husbandry, and thus while their age of improved morality will open with a general robbery, their age of felicity will open with a famine.

Do they intend that the tenure of those

who are to hold the land under the State shall be secure? If they do, nothing will have been gained; private property, and what, to excite odium, they call monopoly, though there are hundreds of thousands of proprietors, will return under another form. The only result of their grand reform will be a change of the name from freeholder to something expressive of concession in perpetuity by the State; and this will be obtained at the expense of a shock to agricultural industry, the probable effect of which, as has been already said, would be a famine. Nothing so practical as a plan for effecting the change without ruinous disturbance appears ever to have entered their minds. But the truth is, that some of them almost openly revel in the prospect of widespread mischief.

When we talk of Nationalizing, it is well to remember, that though territory is still national, nations no longer live upon the produce of their own territory alone, and that the scope of plans of change must be enlarged so as to embrace the commercial world.

A milder school of agrarian socialists proposes to confiscate only what it calls the unearned increment of land—that is, any additional value which, from time to time, may accrue through the action of surrounding circumstances and the general progress of the community, without exertion or outlay on the part of the individual owner. Very sharp and skilful inspectors would be required to watch the increase and to draw the line. A question might also arise, whether, if unearned increment is to be taken away, accidental decrement ought not to be made good. But here, again, we must ask, why landed property alone is to be treated in this way? Property of any kind may grow more valuable without effort or outlay on the owner's part. Is the State to seize upon all the premium on stocks? A mechanic buys a pair of boots, the next day leather goes up; is the State to take toll of the mechanic's boots?

The fact is, that the vision of certain economists is distorted, and their views are narrowed by hatred of the landlord class. Too many landlords are idle and useless members of society, especially in old countries, under the operation of lingering feudal laws; but owners of other kinds of hereditary property are often idle and useless too. That the land should have been so improved as to be able to pay the owner as well as the cultivator, does the community no harm. This we see plainly, where the owner, instead of being a rich man, is a charitable institution. Nor, is any outcry raised, when the same person, being owner and cultivator, unites with the wages

of one the revenue of the other. The belief that there is some evil mystery in rent,
has been fostered by the metaphysical dis-
quisitions of economists, who seem to have
been entrapped by their ignorance of any
language but one. Rent is nothing but the
hire of land, and there is no more mystery
about it than there is about the hire of a
machine or a horse. In Greek, the word for
the hire of land and of a chattel is the same.

The desire of confiscating the property of
landowners is, in European countries, closely
connected with the objects of political revolution. But public spoliation, though it might
commence, would not end here, nor would
there be any ground for fixing this as its
limit. Let a reason be given for confiscating
real estate and the same reason will hold good
for confiscating personal estate, the laborer's
wages, and, we may add, the copyright of the

author and the plant of the journalist who courts popularity or panders to envious malig- nity by advocating the pillage of his neighbor. If property is theft, the property in the Savings Bank is theft like the rest.

Peasant proprietorship is as much opposed as anything can possibly be to nationalization of land. So the Nationalizers, when they approach the peasant proprietor, speedily find. But there are some who look to it with unbounded hope. The political arguments in its favor are well known; among them is the adamantine resistance which it offers to communism of all kinds. Economical considerations are fatally against it, since a farmer on the great scale in Dakota will raise as much grain with a hundred laborers as is raised by ten times the number of French peasants. Socially there are arguments both ways; but the life of the peasant in France, and even in

Switzerland, is hard, and almost barbarous,
while he can scarcely tide over a bad harvest
without falling into the money-lender's hands.
On this continent, where the people are more
educated, their tendency seems to be, when
they can, to exchange life on the farm, which
they find dull and lonely, for the more social
life of the city. Perhaps the time may come
when agriculture will be carried on scientifi-
cally, and upon a large scale, to furnish food
for an urban population. The life of the staff
on a great farm will not be unsocial, while
it will exercise far higher intelligence than
does spade labor, which, in truth, calls for
no intelligence at all.

Liberation of labor from the extortion of
the capitalist is the hope of those who set
on foot co-operative works. These have hitherto
failed from inability to wait for the market,

and tide over bad times, from want of a guid-
ing hand, and from the unwillingness of the
artisan to resign his independence and his
liberty of moving from place to place; though
the last cause is less operative with the sociable
and submissive Frenchman than with his sturdy
English compeer. Capital, spelt with a big
initial letter, swells into a malignant giant—
the personal enemy of labor; spelt in the
natural way, it is simply that with which labor
starts on any enterprise, and without which
no labor can start at all, unless it be that of
the savage grubbing roots with his nails. It
includes a spade as well as factory plant that
has cost millions; it includes everything laid
out in education or training. We might as
well talk of emancipating ourselves from the
tyranny of food or air. Every co-operative
association must have some capital to begin
with, either of its own or borrowed, the lender,

in the latter case, representing the power of large capital just as much as any employer. The aggregation of great masses of capital in one man's hands is a social danger, and one against which legislators ought, by all fair means, to guard, though it is sometimes not without a good aspect; witness the New York Central Railroad, which could hardly have been brought to its present state by managers under the necessity of providing an equally large dividend every year. But the operation of the joint-stock principle, it seems, is evidently pro- ducing a gradual change in this respect. It will often be found that the rate of profit made by a great capitalist is far from excessive, though his total gains may be large. Mr. Brassey's total gains were large, but the rate of his profits did not exceed five per cent, while it is very certain that without him ten thousand workmen, destitute of capital, scientific skill, and powers of command, could not have built the Victoria Bridge. Co-operative farming seems to hold out more hope than co-operative manufactures. Still it would need capital and a head.

To get rid of competition, and substitute for it fraternity among workers, is the other aim of co-operation. But the co-operative societies must compete with each other, while, as buyers, having regard to cheapness in their purchases, they will themselves be always ratifying the principle of competition, and, at the same time, that of paying the workman not on the fraternal principle, but according to the amount and value of his work. Every heart must be touched by fraternity. and wish that co-operation could take the place of competition, which, in its grinding severity, is too like many other things in this hard world. But, after all, choose any manufactured article; consider the multi-

tude of people who in various trades and different countries have co-operated in the production, yet have not competed with each
other; and you will see that, even as things are,
there is more of co-operation than of competition among the workers.

Co-operative stores have nothing but a mis-
leading name in common with co-operative
works. They simply bring the consumer into
direct relation with the producer, and give him
the benefit of wholesale prices, which may be
perfectly well done, so long as the officers of
the association can be trusted to exercise for
the society the same degree of skill and integrity in the selection of goods which the
retail tradesman exercises for himself. Stores,
however, of the ordinary kind, but on a large
scale, like that of A. T. Stewart, with low
prices, and, best of all, ready-money payment,
afford the practical benefits of co-operation.

From Unionism and strikes, again, too much
has been hoped by the workingman. They
have not seldom been the means of enabling
him to make a fairer bargain with the Master,
and they are perfectly lawful; though, the community, to save itself from Unionist tyranny and
extortion; must steadfastly guard the liberties of
the Non-Union men. But the idea that they
can, to an unlimited, or, even, to a great extent
raise wages, is unfounded. The screw may be
put upon the Master, but it cannot be put
upon the community; and it is the community, not the Master, that is the real employer.
The community which buys the goods ulti-
mately settles the price, and, thereby, finally
determines the wages of the producers, not-
withstanding any momentary extortion; nor
can it be constrained, by striking, in the end
to give a cent more than it chooses and can
afford. By strikes, carried beyond a certain

point, capital may be driven away, and the trade may be ruined—as trades have been ruined—but the rate of wages will not be raised. The Master, though commonly taken for the employer, is the agent through whom the community pays the workmen. Towards the men, his commercial relation is really that of a partner, taking out of the earnings of the business the share which is due for capital, risk, and guidance. Masters are beginning to mark this fact in a kindly way, by giving shares in the concern or premiums to the men, while they retain the guidance in their own hands.

Strikers ought to remember that they are, themselves, buyers as well as producers, and, therefore, employers as well as employed; so that if they can strike against the rest of the community, the other trades can strike against them, and wages being thus raised all round, nobody will gain anything. They ought also to remember that they are parts of an industrial organism, on the well-being of which, as a whole, that of all its members depends, and which is deranged, as a˙ whole, by the disturbance of any portion of it. A strike in one section of a trade˳ throws out of work hundreds of men, women, and children, in the other sections. A strike in certain departments, such as that of railways, will stop the wheels of civilization; in others, it will cause incalculable loss and suffering. Suppose, when an artisan had been hurt by the machinery, the surgeons were to˙ put˳ their heads out of the window and say they were on strike. Artisans are in the habit of speaking of themselves exclusively as workingmen. Everybody who is not idle is a workingman, whether he works with his brain or with his hands and whatever part he may play in the service of a varied and complex civilization.

Then, there is the hope of vastly increasing the wealth of the world in general, and
that of the artisans in particular, by means
of an inconvertible Paper Currency. Of this
illusion, it may be said, that not even the
wildest dreams of the alchemist, or of those
adventurers who sailed in quest of an Eldo-
rado, were a more extraordinary instance of
the human power of self-deception. Among
the champions of paper currency there are,
no doubt, knaves—many a one—who know
very well what they are about, and whose
aim is to defraud the creditor, public and
private, by paying off the debt with depre-
ciated paper, an operation, the sweetness of
which, under the Legal Tender Act, has been
already tasted. But there are also honest
enthusiasts, not a few, who sincerely believe
that a commercial millenium could be opened
by merely issuing a flood of promissory notes

and refusing payment. This prodigious fallacy has its origin simply in the equivocal use of a word. We have got into the habit of applying the name money to paper bank bills as well as to coin. The paper bill, being current as well as the coin, we fancy that with both alike we buy goods. But the truth is that we buy only with the coin, to which, alone, the name money ought to be applied. The bank bill is like a cheque—not money itself, but an order and a security for a sum of money, which, the bill being payable on demand, can be drawn by the holder from the bank, or the government, when he pleases. When a man receives a bank bill, he has virtually so much gold as the bill represents put to his account at the bank by which the bill is issued. The bill is a promissory note, and the bank in increasing the number of its bills, like a trader who increases the number of his promissory notes, adds, not to its assets, but to its liabilities.

In the slip of paper itself there is no value or purchasing power; nor can any legislature put value or purchasing power into it.   Green-backers point to the case of postage stamps' into which, they say, value has been put by legislation.   But a postage stamp is simply a receipt for a certain sum paid to the gov. ernment in gold, and, in consideration of which, the government undertakes 'to carry the letter to which the receipt is affixed.

No paper money, it is believed, has ever yet been issued except in the promissory form, pledging the issuer to pay in gold, upon demand, so that each bill, hitherto, has borne upon the face of it a flat denial and abjuration of the Greenback theory.   Suppose the promissory form to be discarded, and the bill to be simply inscribed " one dollar," as the

Fiat-money men propose, what would "dollar" mean? It would mean, say the Greenbackers, a certain proportion of the wealth of the country, upon which, as an aggregate, the currency would be based. What proportion? Let us know what we have in our purse, and what we can get or exchange for the paper dollar on presenting it at a store; otherwise commerce cannot go on. This, however, is not the most serious difficulty. The most serious difficulty is that while the coin, which a convertible bank bill represents, is the property of the bank of issue, the aggregate wealth of the country is not the property of the Government, but of a multitude of private owners. The Government is the possessor of nothing except the public domain, and a taxing power, the exercise of which it is bound to confine to the actual necessities of the State. In issuing an order for a loaf of bread, a coat, or a leg of mutton, to be taken from the possessions of the community at large, it would be simply signing a ticket of spoliation.

Ask the Fiat-money men whether they are prepared to take their own money for taxes, and you will get an ambiguous reply. Some of them have an inkling of the fatal truth, and answer that the taxes must be paid in gold. The faith of others is more robust. But it has been reasonably inquired why the government if it can with a printing machine coin money at its will should pester citizens for taxes at all.

That the foreigner will take the national fiat-money, nobody seems to pretend. Yet, if there is real value in it, why should he not? All the better, say the Greenbackers; if he will not take our money, he will have to take our goods. Then, you will have to take his goods, and the commercial world will be reduced again to barter without a common measure of value, which would not be a great advance in convenience or in civilization. Besides, trade is not merely a direct interchange of commodities between two countries; it is circulation of them among all countries—the United States sending cotton to England, England, calico to China, and China, tea to the United States, which, without a common standard of value, would be next to impossible.

In one sense, of course, government can, by its fiat, put value into paper. It can make the paper Legal Tender for debts—in other words, it can issue licenses of repudiation, and these licenses will retain a value till all existing debts have been repudiated, and all existing creditors cheated; but, from that time their value will cease, since everybody, from the moment of their issue, will refuse to advance money, or sell on credit.

In all the cases known to economical history in which governments have issued in-convertible paper, depreciation has ensued, and such value as it has retained, has been ex actly in proportion to the hope of resump-tion. When cash payments were suspended in England, at the crisis of the French war, the depreciation was comparatively small, simply because the hope of resumption was strong. The guillotine was plied in vain to arrest the rapid fall of French Assignats, though these were not fiat money, but bonds secured on the national domains, which were good secur-ity for the original issue. Confederate paper money, with the defeat of the Confederacy, lost the whole of its value, or retained a shadow of it only, through stock-jobbing tricks. In San Domingo, a gentleman having tendered a silver American dollar in payment for his coffee, received from the surprised and de-lighted keeper of the coffee-house an armful of paper change. Washington, while he was saving his country, was being robbed through the operation of inconvertible paper currency of part of his private estate; and the effects, moral and political, as well as commercial, of the system, during the Revolutionary war, were such that Tom Paine, no timid or squeamish publicist, recommended that death should be made the penalty of any proposal to renew it. In all cases where specie payment has been resumed, the State, in addition to the loss incurred through disturbance and demoralization of commerce, has paid heavily for the temporary suspension, because its credit has been suspended at the same time, and it has had to borrow on terms far worse than those which it could have obtained in the money market, had its integrity been preserved.

The value is in the gold. It is in exchange for the gold that, whenever a sale takes place, the commodity is given.   Trade was originally barter, and, in the sense of being always an interchange of things deemed really equivalent in value, it is barter still.   I give a cow for three sheep, and then give the three sheep for a horse, which it is my ultimate object to purchase.   What the three sheep here do in a single transaction, is done in transactions generally by gold.   This fundamental and vital fact is obscured by the language even of some economists who are sound in principle, but who speak of the precious metals as though their value was conventional, and like that of symbols or counters.   It is nothing of the kind. The first man who gave anything in exchange for gold or silver, must have done so because he deemed gold or silver really valuable; so does the last.   The precious metals, probably, attracted at first by their beauty, their rarity, and their intrinsic qualities; then, they were

felt to have special advantages as mediums
of exchange and universal standards of value,
on account of their durability, their uniformity,
their portability, their capability of receiving -
a stamp, of being divided with exactness, and
of being fused again with ease. Thus they,
and, in the upshot, gold, displaced all the
other articles, such as copper, iron, leather,
shells, which, in primitive times, or under
pressure of circumstances, were adopted as
mediums of exchange and standards of value.
But they have now the additional value de-
rived from immemorial and immutable pre-
scription, which would render it practically
impossible to oust them, even if a substance,
promising greater advantages for the purpose,
could be found. The French Republicans tried
to change the era, and make chronology begin
with the first year of the Republic, instead
of beginning with the birth of Christ. But

they found that they were pulling at a tree, the roots of which were too completely entwined with all existing customs and ideas, to be torn up. It would not be less difficult to change the medium of exchange and standard of value over the whole commercial world. A value which is moral, or dependent on opinion, is not the less real; the value of diamonds, as symbols of wealth and rank, may be dependent, not only on opinion, but on fancy, yet, it is real so long as it lasts. An enormous find of gold would, of course, by putting an end to its rarity, destroy its value; this is a risk which commerce runs, but it does not seem to be great. Any inconvenience that might arise from the bulk and weight of the precious metals, is indefinitely diminished, while in use they are vastly, and in an increasing degree, economized by the employment of bank bills and other paper securities, for gold, which are currency, though money they are not.

There ought to be no such thing as Legal Tender, even in the case of convertible paper currency, either on the part of the government or on the part of private banks. It is rank injustice to compel us to take anybody's paper as gold. If the government is solvent and its security is good, the paper is sure to be taken in preference to carrying about a weight of specie. Legal Tender confuses the ideas of the people, shakes commercial morality, and prepares the way for the attempts of the Fiat-money men, and for all the mischief which they breed.

The last ditch of Greenbackism is Bimetallism, or the proposal to place silver on a par, as a standard, with gold, which can hardly fail to commend itself to Silver Kings. To

force people to take silver for gold, would be
to rob them of the difference; and such a
measure, if adopted by the State, would be
a partial repudiation. Equity would require
that the salaries of all politicians should, first
of all, be paid in the baser metal. To have
two standards is to have none. But it is
proposed that a convention of nations shall
be called to fix the relation of value between
gold and silver. How is it possible for any
convention of nations to fix, and to keep fixed,
the relation of any two commodities, when,
among other determining circumstances, the
rate of production varies from year to year?
This is the problem, without a practical solu-
tion of which it is useless to waste any more
thought upon the question. A great number
of different articles, as has been already said,
have been used from time to time by tribes
or nations, as mediums of exchange and stand-

ards of value; but the choice of the commercial world gradually settled down upon gold,- which is now the medium and standard of the great trading communities, silver being used as change. India and China adhere to silver, as some more barbarous races adhere to cowries or wampum, and to their custom commerce has, in dealing with them, to bend— not without very great inconvenience, as any one who has watched Anglo-Indian finance must know. So long as silver is used only as change, a rough equivalent is sufficient. To ask communities whose wealth is stored in gold to go into convention for the purpose of depreciating gold by reducing it to the level of silver, is to presume upon a blindness, or weakness, seldom found in commercial minds. The movement, accordingly, appears to make but little way.

With belief in Fiat-money are often combined fancies about the tyranny of banks, and
a desire to wreck and plunder them by an
exercise of the legislative power, or to seize
their business and profits, and place them in the
hands of the government. There is nothing,
indeed, of which the demagogues are fonder
than attacking the banks, and they are able,
in this case, to appeal with effect to popular
envy—always the breath of the demagogue's
life. Especially they propose to take away
the circulation of bank bills, and the profits
belonging to it.

Banks are vital organs of a commercial community, which, in seeking their destruction,
would show as much wisdom as a man would
show in seeking the destruction of his own
heart or lungs. They perform for us three indispensable functions, of which the first is the
safe-keeping of our money, which, otherwise, we

should have to keep in our houses at our own risk, as is still the practice of the ignorant French peasant, who hides his hoard in a hole in the wall. The second function is that of economizing gold, and at the same time sparing us the inconvenience of carrying about a mass of specie, by issuing bank bills, which, being secured upon the whole estate of a chartered corporation, may, in general, be accepted without scrutiny, and thus form a paper currency, though it can never be too often repeated that they are not money. It is rather hard that those who are always declaiming against metallic money for its cumbrousness, and because, as they say, it lies dead and inert, should fail to acknowledge the service rendered by the banks of issue, in thus giving the metal wings, and making it do its work for commerce in a thousand places, while it is locally laid up in one. The third function, which is the offspring of comparatively modern times, is that of enabling us to trade on credit. This, the banks do, by discounting paper for the trader, whose resources they have examined, or are assured of, and whose commercial character they approve. In this way, they both substantiate and regulate credit, neither of which could be done without their agency, merely by the representations of the trader himself, or by private inquiry into his means. To stop the action of the banks in this department, would be to render trading on credit impossible, to arrest all enterprise, and to bring the world back to that state of commercial barbarism which, in truth, seems to be the goal of the economical destructives.

The financial Nihilist grudges the banks the profits of their circulation, and wishes to transfer them to that which he calls the State, but which it is necessary always to bear in mind is, in fact, simply the men who compose the government. Why not grudge the banks the profits of the discount business, and propose to transfer that to government in the same way? Why not do the same with all other trades by which profit, and often unfair profit, is made? Why not make the issuing of bills of exchange, or promissory notes; why not make the supplying of the community with boots or dry goods; a monopoly in the hands of the government? What is there about the money trade in particular to make us desire that it should be put into the power of the politicians?   Judging by experience, it would be about the last branch of commerce on which we should wish them to lay their grasp.

It is the business of government to put its stamp on the coin, in order to assure the community that the coin is of the right weight and fineness. This public authorities alone can satisfactorily do, and they may now be trusted to do it, though, in former times, kings were in the habit of defrauding the subject by debasing the coin, a proceeding which combined the guilt of theft with that of forgery. But here the duty and the usefulness of government in regard to the currency end. The volume of bank bills issued ought to be regulated, like that of all other commercial paper, by the requirements of the day—that is, by the number and amount of the transactions, and it will be so regulated while it is in the hands of the banks, which will not fail to issue all the bills for which there is real need, while, if they issue more than are needed, the bills will begin to come back upon their hands. But government can no more decide what amount of bills is required than it can decide how many promissory notes or bills of exchange ought, at any given moment, to be afloat. Setting government to settle the circulation of paper, is having the barometer regulated by superior wisdom without reference to atmospheric pressure.

The English Bank Charter Act was the offspring of the alarm caused by the failure of a number of private banks of issue. It would have been better to adopt proper safeguards in the way of inspection and other precautionary regulations. The Act has gone into operation only to a limited extent, having put an end to the existence of a few only of the private banks of issue, all of which it was intended gradually to extinguish. It has been three times suspended at a commercial crisis, each suspension being attended with all the inconvenience and injustice of arbitrary intervention; and its general effect, whenever tightness is felt, is to produce a sort of nervous contraction, which itself tends to the acceleration of a crisis. It ought not to be forgotten that the Bank of England, though employed by the government, is quite a distinct institution ; while, in England, the commercial interest is so strong that no politician in power could venture to tamper with the bank or its operations. Once more the working of an economical measure depends partly on the circumstances of the country.

Ordinary banks, being private institutions, are amenable to the law: in truth, there is nothing of which the politicians are fonder than harassing and oppressing them with legislation. But a party government, supported by a majority, is its own law, and can do whatever its need or its cupidity inspires, without regard to the interests of commerce. Even the least dishonest of such governments, when in want of money, thanksnothing of issuing a flood of legal tender currency, without reference to the state of the money market, a proceeding which is in the nature of a forced loan. Would commerce have an hour of security, or be able to conduct

any of her operations in peace and confidence,
if the hand of demagogism were all the time
upon her heartstrings ?

Bank bills, though not legal tender, cannot,
in the ordinary course of trade, be 'refused,
unless there is some public reason for mistrust-
ing the solvency of the bank. This is the
ground for subjecting this particular class of
commercial companies to special legislation;
and it is the sole ground; there would, otherwise, be no justification for an interference with
the trade in money more than with any other
trade. Nor has the government the slightest
right to compel the banks to take its bonds, as
the condition of permitting them to pursue an
honest and indispensable traffic, or to blackmail
them in any other way. To do so is confiscation, and upon confiscation retribution never
fails to attend. It is not the bank, but
the demagogue, that on this continent is the

pest of industry, as well as of public affairs and morality in general. On the other hand, the stockholders of banks must not suppose that they, of all investors in commercial enterprises, are entitled to the intervention of government when their affairs are mismanged by directors of their own choosing. If they invoke such aid, they will once more practically point the moral of the fable of the horse and the stag.

The notion that society is an organism or growth has perhaps been carried too far; we have an individuality and a power of acting on the general frame, which the parts of an organism have not. But this view is, at least, nearer the truth than the fancy which underlies all Socialism, that society can be completely meta- morphosed by the action of the State—an imaginary power outside all personalities, superior to all special interests, and free from all class passions. Nothing, indeed, can be less free from class passions than the movements which have been here passed in review. Social hatred is a bad reformer, and the struggles to which it has given birth have almost always brought to the community, and even to the most suffering members of it, ten times as much loss as gain.

To speak of Protection, would be opening a wide subject, and one which, perhaps, scarcely falls within the scope of this paper. There are men, sensible in other things, who imagine that they can increase the wealth of a country by taxation. So long as governments and armaments are maintained on the present scale of expenditure, every country will need import duties, and must have its tariff. Absolute free trade, therefore, is at present out of the question, and the different tariffs must be regulated according to the circumstances and the special industries of each community. Every nation will claim this right. England, who has her tariff like the rest, wisely lets in free the raw materials of her special industries and the food of her innumerable workmen, while she taxes finished articles of, luxury, such as tea, wine and tobacco. Free traders, British free traders, especially, have left this too much out of sight, and have compromised their theory by that error. But, that taxation can add to wealth; that governments can increase production by forcing capital and labor out of their natural channels; that the interest of the people will be promoted by forbidding them to buy the best and cheapest article wherever it can be found; are notions which, if reason did not sufficiently confute them, have been confuted by experience. Under the free system, the industries of England have been developed, and her wealth has increased out of all proportion to the growth of her population, and to an-extent perfectly unrivalled. The verdict of economical history through all the ages is the same. Nobody proposes to draw Customs lines across the territory of any nation, and the commercial advantages of freedom of exchange know no political limit, though in passing from nation to nation, fiscal necessity intervenes. The workman does not gain by Protection; he is only transferred to an artificial industry from a natural industry, which would otherwise develop itself, and in which, as it would be more remunerative, employment would be more abundant. The master manufacturer is the only man who gains; to him the community, under the Protective system, pays tribute; accordingly, he is generally a Protectionist, and uses not argument alone, but the Lobby, and influences of all sorts, to keep up the tariff; he will do his utmost to encourage national expenditure, rather than taxes shall go⁻ down. Nor can he be much blamed, when the government has induced him to put his capital into the favored trade, and stake his future on the continuance of the favor. Political or social motives there may conceivably be for Protection, as well as for any other sacrifice of commercial interest, such as war itself; but the commercial sacrifice is a fact which cannot be denied. To foster by protective duties or bonuses infant industries, which may afterwards sustain themselves, and perhaps draw emigration to a new country, is in itself a perfectly rational and legitimate policy, if the nation can really keep the experiment in its own hands. But artificial interests are created, a Ring is formed, and the nation loses control over its tariff. Such, at least, is the case with communities governed as are those of this continent; and again, in concluding, we would strive to impress the necessity of regarding the field of political economy as a region not in the air but on the earth, and of treating the society with which the economical legislator deals, its tendencies, its capabilities and its forces, as they really are. The connection of political economy with politics is a blank page in the treatises of the great writers.

Steady industry aided by the ever-growing powers of practical science is rapidly augmenting wealth. Thrift, increased facilities for saving and for the employment of small capitals will promote equality of distribution. Let governments see that labor is allowed to enjoy its full earnings, untaxed by war, waste or protective tariffs. For the unfortunate, of whom, in a great community, however prosperous, there must always be some, charity, which is daily becoming more active and bountiful, will provide.

www.ingramcontent.com/pod-product-compliance
Lightning Source LLC
Chambersburg PA
CBHW021532270326
41930CB00008B/1215